**Level 1** is ideal for some initial reading i_ very simply, using a s_ repeated words.

## Special features:

Opening pages introduce key story words

Careful match between story and pictures

Large, clear type

**Educational Consultant: Geraldine Taylor**
**Book Banding Consultant: Kate Ruttle**

A catalogue record for this book is available from the British Library

Published by Ladybird Books Ltd
80 Strand, London, WC2R 0RL
A Penguin Company

004
© LADYBIRD BOOKS LTD MMX. This edition MMXIV
Ladybird, Read It Yourself and the Ladybird Logo are registered or
unregistered trademarks of Ladybird Books Limited.

All rights reserved. No part of this publication may be reproduced,
stored in a retrieval system, or transmitted in any form or by any means,
electronic, mechanical, photocopying, recording or otherwise,
without the prior consent of the copyright owner.

ISBN: 978-0-72327-270-0

Printed in China

# Little Red Hen

Illustrated by Virginia Allyn

Little Red Hen

The rat

The bread

The flour

"Will you help me
plant the wheat?"
asked Little Red Hen.

"No," said the rat,
the cat and the dog.

"Then I will plant it all by myself," said Little Red Hen.

And she did.

"Then I will cut it all by myself," said Little Red Hen.

And she did.

"Will you help me make the flour?" asked Little Red Hen.

"No," said the rat, the cat and the dog.

"Then I will make it all by myself," said Little Red Hen.

And she did.

"Will you help me
make the bread?"
asked Little Red Hen.

"No," said the rat,
the cat and the dog.

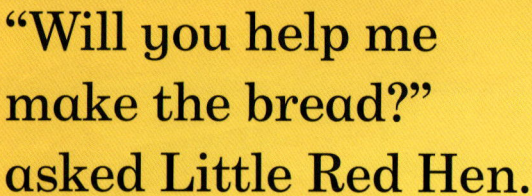

"Then I will make it all by myself," said Little Red Hen.

And she did.

"Will you help me
eat the bread?"
asked Little Red Hen.

"Yes," said the rat, the cat and the dog.

"No," said Little Red Hen.
"I will eat it all by myself."

And she did!

How much do you remember about the story of Little Red Hen? Answer these questions and find out!

- Who does Little Red Hen ask to help her?

- What do they do instead of helping her?

- What does Little Red Hen eat all by herself?